Robert Willrich

The Depiction of Class and Self-

Robert Willrich

The Depiction of Class and Self-Created Identity in "The Buddha of Suburbia"

GRIN Verlag

Bibliografische Information der Deutschen Nationalbibliothek: Die Deutsche Bibliothek verzeichnet diese Publikation in der Deutschen Nationalbibliografie; detaillierte bibliografische Daten sind im Internet über http://dnb.d-nb.de/ abrufbar.

1. Auflage 2009
Copyright © 2009 GRIN Verlag
http://www.grin.com/
Druck und Bindung: Books on Demand GmbH, Norderstedt Germany
ISBN 978-3-640-54293-2

Robert Willrich

The Depiction of Class and Self-Created Identity in *The Buddha of Suburbia*

The Depiction of Class and Self-Created Identity in *The Buddha of Suburbia*

Table of Contents

1 INTRODUCTION

Being one of Hanif Kureishi's most famous works, *The Buddha of Suburbia* has been discussed numerously in academic writing. Up to now, most scholars have, unfortunately, only focussed on the most apparent topics of hybridity and racial as well as migrational identity. Although fairly striking, only few have paid attention to the British class system that is portrayed in the novel, and if they have, only in passing.

This paper is not intended to be added to this long list. I rather want to concentrate on how diverse and comprehensively the topic of class is approached by Kureishi, how class is depicted. For this reason, I want start with some more general facts about lower middle class, but will try to directly compare them to the contents of *The Buddha of Suburbia*.

Secondly, I aim to show how, especially, class is depicted and to describe what makes someone belong to a certain class. How is affiliation expressed and how can one distinguish from other social groups? What does influence our thoughts and beliefs, and why do people want to break out? In regard to this, I will pay special attention to how the suburbs are presented in the novel and to what extent they differ from London.

Finally, I want to examine in how far London offers a chance to flee suburbia and lower middle class influences. Does the anonymity of England's capital provide the basis for a new self, to create something new, and leave the past behind? Do people have to surrender, not to say sacrifice, their old identities in order to make it in London? What is the price for climbing the social ladder, and can one find a new, but genuine, self after having left the old behind?

My paper shall answer these questions, it seeks to unfold some of the complexity of Kureishi's début novel and to offer a new approach for interpreting *The Buddha of Suburbia*.

2 LOWER MIDDLE CLASS IN BRITAIN AND ITS PORTRAYAL IN THE *BUDDHA OF SUBURBIA*

In order to understand the *Buddha of Suburbia* to its full extend, it is indispensable to completely comprehend the British class system as »the term ›social class‹ has a good deal of currency among the [British] population at large and that they are prepared to use it of themselves.«[1] Its importance, even still today, derives from the belief that a person's class-belonging affects one's opportunities in society.[2] When reading Kureishi's novel, the recipient will become aware that topics concerned with the British class system arise constantly – especially subjects dealing with lower and upper middle class.

Lower middle class does not enjoy much prestige in academic writing. It is said to be »the social class with the lowest reputation in the entire history of class theory [...], the class for whom it seems hardest [...] to claim pride of membership«.[3] Furthermore, it is seen as a rather negative identity, »a category usually applied from outside, by those of higher social status, or retrospectively, by those who once belonged to the lower middle class and have since moved beyond it.«[4] If it is not perceived in this dismissive way, at least, lower middle classness is understood as a non-identity.[5] Looking for an identity of their own, Karim and Charlie would prove this judgement in *The Buddha of Suburbia* as both of them endeavor to belong to another social group: The latter attempts to join the newly founded and morbid punk movement, whereas Karim, in contrast, aims to raise his social status by becoming an actor.

Social mobility enables the protagonists to perform this migration of status and prestige, and signifies that class is not a fixed construct. Two varieties of social mobility are commonly acknowledged: intra-generational and inter-generational mobility.[6] Both of them are represented to us in Kureishi's novel. Haroon and – as the name implies already – Princess Jeeta, for example, were born into a high caste back in India. After they had gone to England, their social status had declined dramatically. The social

---

1   Ivan Reid, *Class in Britain* (Malden, Mass.: Polity Press, 1998), 32.
2   Cf. Reid, *Class in Britain*, 33.
3   John Hartley, *Popular Reality: Journalism, Modernity, Popular Culture* (London: Arnold, 1996), 161.
4   Rita Felski, »Nothing to Declare: Identity, Shame, and the Lower Middle Class.« *Publications of the Modern Language Association of America* 115.1 (2000): 41.
5   Felski, »Nothing to Declare«, 34.
6   Cf. Reid, *Class in Britain*, 111.

development from the lower middle class »English« Haroon to his upper middle class son Karim, in contrast, marks an inter-generational one.

When in Britain increasingly more labour was needed to be done in offices, some men started taking jobs as clerks and secretaries. Working in these positions was acceptable for most of the men, but they did not consider it appropriate for their sons to have a similar occupation. That is why only very few boys whose fathers were occupied in a non-manual profession entered this kind of job themselves.[7] Haroon, too, does not want his son to be a clerk working in an office as he does, but rather to pursue the aim of being a doctor.[8] It was more often women taking on jobs with ›feminine‹ tasks such as customer care.[9] Working as a sales assistant in a shoe shop, even Margaret, Karim's mother, fits into that pattern perfectly fine. Thus, there cannot be any doubt that the Amirs constitute a typical lower middle class family.

Nevertheless, it is not only white-collar workers that account for the whole lower middle class. Usually, the petit bourgeois belongs to this social group, too, and includes »[…] shopkeepers, garages, builders [and] other service businesses […].«[10] These small businesses are mostly dominated by men. Over four-fifths of the self-employed are male.[11] This resembles exactly what is portrayed in The Buddha of Suburbia: The only two people belonging to the petit bourgeois we become acquainted with are Anwar and Karim's uncle, Ted. The former is the proprietor of a small grocer's shop (cf. BoS 26), the latter runs a central heating business (cf. BoS 33). Being predominantly male, the self-employed also »pride themselves on masculine values such as competitiveness, independence and individualism.«[12] In the Buddha this becomes apparent by the parties Ted and Jean had given in the heydays of »Peter's Heaters« because they were »a little king and queen in those days – rich, powerful, influential« (BoS 42), and their guests were the »most important builders, bank managers, accountants, local politicians and businessmen […] with their wives and tarts.« (BoS 41) Ted was definitely more successful with his business than Anwar although both of them have a »work-centred lifestyle: they work long ours, and homes are usually workplaces«.[13] This is even more

---

7 Kenneth Roberts, Class in Modern Britain (Basingstoke: Palgrave, 2001), 130.
8 Hanif Kureishi, The Buddha of Suburbia (London: Faber and Faber, 1990), 23. In the following abbreviated as BoS. All subsequent quotations of the Buddha are taken from this edition.
9 Roberts, Class in Modern Britain, 132.
10 Roberts, Class in Modern Britain, 135.
11 Roberts, Class in Modern Britain, 136.
12 Roberts, Class in Modern Britain, 136.
13 Roberts, Class in Modern Britain, 138.

true for Anwar: He works very close to where he lives and spends most of his time in his shop. If Ted did the same before he stopped working, we can only guess. From his former success, however, we can infer that he must have been fairly industrious.

There is also another point about the petit bourgeois in Kureishi's novel that portrays British life very precisely because in »terms of ethnic mix, the self-employed are less dominated by whites than any other class. Indians, Pakistanis and Bangladeshis are overrepresented [...]. Britain's ethnic minorities have transformed the restaurant trade, and have also made a major impact in retailing.«[14] Anwar is a perfect example for this influence of the ›black‹ on British society. Being usually not discriminated like other immigrants, Indians and Pakistanis can be seen as assimilated into British culture.[15] This is the main reason why I will not focus on racial discrimination or racial identity in my paper, but rather deal with Karim and his family as British citizens. Besides, »Kureishi's London, with its ›thousands of blacks‹, is internally influenced by the culture of minorities as well as by emergent cultural groups like the punk movement.«[16] Therefore, Karim must not be seen as a foreigner, but as British, especially since he was born in the United Kingdom and has never been to India. Of course, the rule of living in a diverse metropolis does not prove right for all the time of his life. Having grown up in the London suburb of Bromley, Karim had to face narrow-mindedness at first and was, indeed, rather an exception in his neighbourhood as far as skin colour is concerned.[17]

3 THE DEPICTION OF CLASS

3.1 Suburbia

The situation of living in a London suburb is a very distinctive one; it is »as close to the green belts of the Black Country and rural Kent as [it is] to the metropolitan centre[]«.[18] However, being so close to the British capital, the suburbs hold a obvious disadvantage: they will never be anything but peripheral compared to it.[19] Therefore, there is always the lure for something greater, the temptation of the city. The suburbs do not offer

---

14 Roberts, *Class in Modern Britain*, 136.
15 Roberts, *Class in Modern Britain*, 211.
16 Anthony Ilona, »Hanif Kureishi's *Buddha of Suburbia*: ›A New Way of Being British‹«, *Contemporary British fiction*, ed. Richard Lane et al (Cambridge: Polity Press, 2003), 101.
17 Cf. BoS 64: »[T]here were so few Asians in our part of London [...].«
18 James Procter, *Dwelling Places: Postwar Black British Writing* (Manchester: Manchester Univ. Press, 2003), 128.
19 Procter, *Dwelling Places*, 128.

anything, whereas the city seems to have everything a young person is longing for: freedom, dozens of shops and »parties where girls and boys you didn't know took you upstairs and fucked you; there were all the drugs you could use.« (BoS 121)

Karim's expectations are very opposing to his opinion about the suburbs where, according to him, »people rarely dream[] of striking out for happiness« (BoS 8), so that, in the end, their lives are dominated by »dullness« (BoS 8). Bearing that in mind, it is not surprising that Karim's life is characterised by a »claustrophobic anxiety [...] to be ›always somewhere else‹«.[20] For him, Bromley is nothing but a point of departure on his way to the city, »a leaving place, the start of a life.«[21] He was looking for something only London could offer him; he just did not fit into this boring narrow-minded way of living. If he had wanted to fit in, he would have had to play according to certain rules, which was impossible to him.

The very fact alone that he »wanted to sleep with boys as well as with girls« and that to him it would have been »heart-breaking to have to choose one or the other« (BoS 55) made him an outsider where he had lived. This sexual difference, his skin colour, »along with his refusal of fixed identity categories, is often associated with urban cosmopolitanism and seen as a challenge to suburban sameness.«[22] Even though Bromley belongs to Greater London, it is not comparable to the inner city. Bromley is missing everything metropolitan: adventure, discovery, excitement, consumption, indulgence, and from that point of view the outer suburbs cannot be considered ›London‹.[23] Karim himself makes this clear to the reader when introducing London to us: »In London the kids looked fabulous; they dressed and walked and talked like little gods. We could have been from Bombay. We'd never catch up.« (BoS 127 f.) This scene reveals how different both worlds are; Karim appears to be intimidated by the Londoners although he has lived in only a few miles distance from the ›real London‹ for years. He should be familiar with this kind of fashion and their language, and, in fact, one would suspect him not to be different to that at all.

Kureishi, however, goes further than that to create a strong contrast. Not only is it fashion that distinguishes both of Karim's dwelling places, but rather that the suburbs

---

20 Procter, *Dwelling Places*, 62.
21 BoS 117; also cf. Procter, *Dwelling Places*, 150.
22 Susan Brook, »Hedgemony?: Suburban Space in The Buddha of Suburbia,« *British fiction of the 1990s*, ed. Nick Bentley (London: Routledge, 2005), 214 f.
23 John Clement Ball, »The Semi-Detached Metropolis: Hanif Kureishi's London«, *ARIEL (A Review of International English Literature)* 27.4 (1996): 21.

are seen as »safe where the city is dangerous; conformist where the city is heterogenous; monotonous and enervating where the city is diverse and stimulating; the site of heterosexual family life where the city opens up the potential for sexual experimentation and possibility.«[24] All these contrasts become obvious while reading the novel, and I want to further investigate these features.

Brook states that the city is a more dangerous place to live in while the suburbs are more peaceful. Although Karim also gets in trouble in Bromley (cf. »Hairy Back«), the city still appears to be more threatening. In London, Changez »had been attacked under a railway bridge« (BoS 224), and this gang »planted their feet all over him and started to carve the initials of the National Front into his stomach with a razor blade.« (BoS 224) Besides, South London, in general is described as a perilous place where »the housing estates looked like makeshift prison camps; dogs ran around; rubbish blew about« (BoS 224), and Brixton seems even more uncomfortable:

> On my day off I went to see Terry. He and his mates were squatting a house in Brixton. [...] The kids here were wilder than anywhere else in London. [...] The area was full of shebeens, squats, lesbian bars, gay pubs, drug pubs, drug organizations, advice centres, and the offices of various radical political organizations. There wasn't much work going on; people were hanging out; they asked you if you wanted black hash, which I did, but not from them.[25]

These kinds of places have never been described when Karim talked about the suburbs. On the contrary, he refers to Bromley as a place closely connected to »security and safety« (BoS 8). The price for this safety, however, is a conformist and monotonous life, as Brook mentions. We only need to take a closer look at Karim's parents »who went to the pictures maybe once a year« (BoS 46) and especially at Haroon who »polished his shoes [...] with patience and care, every Sunday morning.« (BoS 47) Their son, on the other hand, acquaints himself to innumerable new people and has a job about which he can claim that he had »never been so enthusiastic about anything«; an occupation he perceives as his »big chance, in more ways than one.« (BoS 167) Also, sexual experimentation signals to us that the metropolis is definitely more diverse than suburbia. So, Karim's wish for orgies will become fulfilled in the end, but in a slightly different way than he had in his mind:

---

24 Brook, »Hedgemony«, 209.
25 BoS 238 f.

> Later, when I looked up, [...] Pyke's body was carrying his erection in my direction, like a lorry sustaining a crane. ›That looks fun,‹ his voice said. ›Yes, it –‹ But before I could complete the sentence, England's most interesting and radical theatre director was inserting his cock between my speaking lips.[26]

Unnecessary to mention that, although Karim is bisexual, he did not like this experience very much as »it seemed an imposition« (BoS 203) to him. Having been raised in India and being influenced by a suburban English life style, Haroon, in contrast, represents a purely heterosexual morality which is shown in the fact that he »was so terrified that [Karim] might turn out gay that he could never bring himself to mention the matter [of homosexuality]« (BoS 174) because in his eyes »being a man and denying your male sex was perverse and self-destructive« (BoS 174). When he had spotted Karim kissing Charlie, he even wanted to slap him, called him a »bum-banger« and wanted to have Karim's »balls examined« (BoS 18).

Because of all that the main protagonist feels trapped in this semi-detached[27] lower middle class area which becomes a metonym for parochialism and smallness.[28] Englishness, in general, becomes provincialised by the images established in the novel; ›smallness‹ and the »*ethnicity* of [...] middle-class south London life« is disclosed and satirised.[29] Nevertheless, Karim also belongs to this culture. He is a local, born and raised there and therefore more English than Indian.

3.2 Housing and Appearance

However, most of the values traditionally connected to lower middle class are associated with women: »domesticity, prudery, aspirations toward refinement.«[30] In the *Buddha of Suburbia*, too, it is Margaret, Karim's mother, who is longing for an improvement of the living conditions as she looked »reproachfully at Dad, as if to say: What husband are you to give me so little when the other men, the Alans and Barrys and Peters and Roys, provide cars, houses, holidays, central heating and jewellery?« (BoS 29) Throughout the whole novel, housing seems to be something to

---

26 BoS 202.
27 Although not explicitly mentioned, one can infer that the Amir's live in a semi-detached house (»The Kays [...] had a bigger house, with a little drive and garage and car. Their place stood on its own [...].«, BoS 8).
28 Procter, *Dwelling Places*, 149.
29 Procter, *Dwelling Places*, 128.
30 Rita Felski, »Nothing to Declare«, 43.

construct identity with, an asset that helps to distinguish oneself from one's neighbours and acquaintances. The reader will find mostly women redecorating houses and establishing a sense of self by doing so.[31] Eva even goes so far as making it her profession to refurbish houses and flats. Apart from creating an own self, redecorating the house has another purpose: to stand one's ground against »the invisible gaze of the Neighbourhood Watch.«[32] What CCTV is in public, is the curious neighbour in a more private field. Whereas no one is interested in their neighbours doing in a city, and, in fact, does hardly know the people living next-door, in the suburbs most people know each other and gladly participate in any gossip available to them. Therefore, most women think it necessary to pay attention to their own and their family's behaviour and appearance. Nevertheless, Margaret almost seems to suffer from a persecution complex when she tells her husband off for not dressing properly while doing his yoga exercises.

> »She said to Dad, ›Oh God, Haroon, all the front of you's sticking out like that and everyone can see!‹ She turned to me. ›You encourage him to be like this. At least pull the curtains!‹ ›It's not necessary, Mum. There isn't another house that can see us for a hundred yards – unless they're watching through binoculars.‹ ›That's exactly what they are doing,‹ she said.[33]

When looking at passages like these, Felski must be right when she says that »the lower middle class is driven by the fear of shame [and] tortured by a constant struggle to keep up appearances on a low income.«[34] Margaret, for example, is seeking a better house, a car, »holidays, central heating and jewellery« (BoS 29) although it is not possible as her husband is only »badly paid« (BoS 7) and she does not earn much money either. As this accumulation of luxury is not affordable to them, Margaret, at least, makes sure that the house is always clean and everything, including herself, looks respectable. This becomes especially apparent when Jimmy, her new lover, is about to visit her: »While she [Margaret] showered and dressed, we dusted and vacuumed the front room. [...] Mum spent ages preparing herself, and Allie told her what jewellery to wear, and the right shoes and everything.« (BoS 269) While Margaret's habits are not very outstanding, her sister Jean is definitely more extreme as far as her behaviour is concerned: Standing at the »abyss of bankruptcy« (BoS 102), Jean still tries to keep up her appearance in order not to lose her dignity. When Karim visits his uncle and aunt, Jean was »straight-backed

---

31 Brook, »Hedgemony«, 217.
32 Brook, »Hedgemony«, 209.
33 BoS 4.
34 Felski, »Nothing to Declare«, 35.

and splendid in high heels and a dark-blue dress with a diamond brooch in the shape of a diving fish pinned to her front. Her nails were perfect little bright shells. [...] She seemed ready to attend one of those cocktail parties« (BoS 103). Reading this, it becomes quite clear that Jean tries everything to conceal that she has left her former social rank when Ted and her were »rich, powerful, influential« (BoS 42). Pretending to be someone else is manifested as symptomatic for the lower middle class in the suburbs; the »detached interior is turned into a theatrical setting [...], a locus of ›display‹ and ›exhibition‹ available for a neighbourly tourism, or what Karim's dad ironically refers to as ›the grand tour‹[35].«[36]

For this reason, *DIY* seems to be one of the major keywords in the novel. Having a house in the suburbs means improving, refining and displaying money.

> All of the houses had been ›done up‹. One had a new porch, another double-glazing, ›Georgian‹ windows or a new door with brass fittings. Kitchens had been extended, lofts converted, walls removed, garages inserted. This was the English passion, not for self-improvement or culture or wit, but for DIY, Do It Yourself, for bigger and better houses with more mod cons, the painstaking accumulation of comfort and, with it, status – the concrete display of earned cash.[37]

Most often status, and therefore class, is constituted by our environment, the people next to us, and what they think we are. That is why displaying earned money appears to be so important in these certain areas of Britain. An impressive house distinguishes its dwellers from their neighbours and, consequentially, confers them a higher status.[38] Therefore, suburbanites attempt to look as affluent and as honourable as possible and keep »hoovering, hosepiping, washing, polishing, shining, scraping, repainting, discussing and admiring their cars.« (BoS 39) Unfortunately, most identities are as superficial as the polish on the cars or the paint most suburban walls are covered with. When it comes to identities, the novel privileges surface rather than depth,[39] and reveals that identity is a construct made by their owners: It is not about who we are, but about who we appear to be.

---

35 By referring to this neighbourly tourism as the »grand tour« (BoS 75), Haroon denounces it as a lower middle class version of the Grand Tour wealthy Oxbridge graduates used to do around the 18th century. Rather than a journey through Europe, the suburban Grand Tour only explores neighbouring houses, which reveals in a subtle way how absurd this boastful behaviour is.

36 Procter, *Dwelling Places*, 148.

37 BoS 74 f.

38 Cf. Brook, »Hedgemony«, 217.

39 Brook, »Hedgemony«, 217.

3.3   The Role of Education

Although role-playing turns out to be highly important to most characters, once in a
while a more substantial topic comes up: education. Especially, when Karim is around
Eleanor, he feels inferior to her and her knowledge. He becomes »aware that [he] knew
nothing; [he] was empty, an intellectual void.« (BoS 177) Karim becomes more and more
intimidated by Eleanor and her friends for whom »hard words and sophisticated ideas
were in the air they breathed from birth, and this language was the currency that bought
you the best of what the world could offer. But for us it could only ever be a second
language, consciously acquired.« (BoS 178) »For us« means the kids who had been
raised in the suburbs, the ones who did not »consider[] [education] a particular
advantage« (BoS 177). For these children it was not as natural to do their A-levels and
study at a good university. In fact, most of them were »happily condemning
[themselves] to being nothing better than motor-mechanics« (BoS 178) while thinking
themselves different from the »public school kids, with their puky uniforms and leather
briefcases, and Mummy and Daddy waiting outside in the car to pick them up«
(BoS 178). They were »proud of never learning anything except the names of footballers«
(BoS 178), but now Karim is among people whose »easy talk of art, theatre, architecture,
travel« (BoS 177) infuriated and fascinated him at the same time.

Rita Felski claims that these »bohemian and avant-garde elements of modern art
and criticism remain largely incomprehensible to individuals from a petit bourgeois
cultural milieu.«[40] In my opinion, Felski is right with her statement when we look at the
majority of Karim's classmates. Still, there are some people who manage to go further
than the others, and Karim belongs to one of them. He manages to gain more education
as he is surrounded by upper middle class actors now and as he has read books ever
since. Nonetheless, all this talk about art and books can remain to Karim nothing but a
»second language, consciously acquired.« (BoS 178)

However, if he does not want to attract too much attention, learning how to have a
conversation about modern art or contemporary plays is not the only thing he has to
master: He also needs to leave his accent behind. He has never noticed it himself, it was
Eleanor who pointed it out to him: »›You've got a street voice, Karim. You're from South
London – so that's how you speak. It's like cockney, only not so raw. It's not unusual.
It's different to my voice, of course.‹« (BoS 178) This piece of information is exactly what

---

40 Felski, »Nothing to Declare«, 41.

Karim does not want to hear any longer; he does not want to be ›different‹ from his newly gained environment, not even concerning his language. He tried everything to scour the ›suburban stigma‹ off him, and now he is forced to realise that it has not worked out at all. Consequentially, he »resolve[s] to lose [his] accent«, and that, in the end, he »would speak like her.« (BoS 178) By deciding this, he also determines to totally hide his suburban origin, he does not want to be associated with it anymore – »[He]'d left [his] world« (BoS 178).

3.4 Jobs and Everyday Life

I have already explained that the lower middle class includes the traditional petit bourgeoisie such as shop owners or small businesspeople and what is considered the ›new‹ lower middle class which includes secretaries, technicians, clerical workers and salaried employees.[41] All these occupations »pay little more and often less than blue-collar industrial jobs.«[42] When comparing the Amirs to other families, it becomes obvious that they have less money than other people in their neighbourhood. Karim, for example, mentions that the »Kays were much better off than us, and had a bigger house« (BoS 8). As I have proved before, judging the income of a British family by the house is quite legitimate as it is used to display »earned cash« (BoS 75). Karim tells the reader that his dad »ended up working as a clerk in the Civil Service for £3 a week.« (BoS 26) Haroon left the »rotten place« of India (BoS 64) in order to receive a decent education in England, and, in addition to that, »left a quasi-aristocratic freedom for a workaday prison.«[43] Now he polishes »his shoes […] with patience and care, every Sunday morning. Then he brushe[s] his suits, […] and arrange[s] his ties.« (BoS 47) Not only do his working clothes appear rigid, his daily routine seems exactly the same, and we cannot help but to agree with Karim that Haroon's life »once a cool river of balmy distraction […] [is] now a cage of umbrellas and steely regularity.« (BoS 26) Every working day is the same and as much routine as his shoe polishing on Sundays. Haroon lives in Bromley and works in inner-city London which makes him one of those thousands of commuters representing the ›Unreal City‹ and giving a certain degree of

---

41 Reid, *Class in Britain*, 34 f.
42 Reid, *Class in Britain*, 34 f.
43 Ball, »The Semi-Detached Metropolis«, 23.

inauthenticity to urban life.[44] Except for work, most commuters do not spend much time in London; usually, they »never socialize[] with anyone from the office« but flee »as quickly as they [can] after work.« (BoS 46) It is almost like having two lives: a private and a working life, neither of them interesting, and due to commuting the daily routine is, moreover, »regulated to the minute« (BoS 46).

Yet, it is exactly this rigidity, grey routine and respectability lower middle classness is marked by.[45] Even Allie, Karim's younger brother, who works as a fashion designer, is marked by these influences. It is precisely this dullness he appreciates in his mother's new lover: »Jimmy's OK. He's respectable, he's employed, he doesn't put his prick around.« (BoS 268) There are two details that convince Allie that Jimmy is the right man for his mother: First of all he looks boring enough to not be unfaithful, and, secondly, being employed means he will be able to make ends meet easily.

Rita Felski states that »[f]rugality, decency, and self-discipline, rather than an enthusiasm for Dionysian orgies, have often been the core values of the poor.«[46] Of course, the Amir's financial conditions, although very modest, cannot be considered poor which becomes clear when Karim is on the train watching

the slums of Herne Hill and Brixton, places so compelling and unlike anything [Karim] was used to seeing that [he] jumped up, jammed down the window and gazed out at the rows of disintegrating Victorian houses. The gardens were full of rusting junk and sodden overcoats; lines of washing criss-crossed over the debris.[47]

Although neither poor nor well-off, most of the main protagonists do not show much frugality. In fact, they try to leave their class boundaries behind and to gain a higher social prestige. Karim, Eva, Charlie and Allie want to enjoy Dionysian higher-class pleasures, and refuse, in consequence, Apollonian jobs in order to aim for something more artistic. With everyone trying to fulfil their dreams and searching for an identity of their own, most families are left dysfunctional.[48] Haroon, for example, »leaves his wife sitting at home in the suburbs watching television [...] while he ›buddhas off‹ beyond Bromley with Eva«.[49] Although most of the characters in The Buddha of Suburbia – with the exception of for Margaret, Jean and Ted – seem quite occupied with many different

44 Brook, »Hedgemony«, 211.
45 Felski, »Nothing to Declare«, 37.
46 Felski, »Nothing to Declare«, 35.
47 BoS 43.
48 Janet Wilson, »The Family and Change: Contemporary Second-Generation British-Asian Fiction«, CDS Research Report 23 (2005), 115 f.

activities, some critics deny the lower middle class a social life. Before Haroon, for example, started touring the neighbouring houses, his life was quite a dismal and uneventful one. Him and his wife »went to the pictures maybe once a year, and [he] always fell asleep« (BoS 46). Accordingly, the social life of the lower middle class is regarded »almost nonexistent, since the ubiquitous English pub is considered vulgar, working-class, and hence out-of-bounds.«[50] Having hardly any social life, it is fairly problematic to create an own identity as the prevailing emotion is boredom.[51] However, having no specific identity at all offers a great advantage: one can create one, and London delivers the best conditions for doing so.

4 LONDON: THE CHANCE TO INVENT A NEW SELF

4.1 The Depiction of London

While the suburbs are represented as rather stifling, London is a location of diversity.[52] Everything seems possible and nobody knows what other people are like, London is dominated by anonymity. Thus, it is the perfect basis for display, artifice, performance and spectatorship; in short, it is nothing but a theatrical space.[53] Since in the suburbs everybody knows their neighbours, people can invent a new self only to a certain degree; most of the times it is, in fact, almost impossible. Taking advantage of London's anonymity, in contrast, a person can pretend to be whoever he or she likes. Big city life offers the chance of identity as a mutable concept.[54] When Karim and Charlie moved to London, they were full of excitement and open-minded about everything they were going to experience. Yet, they came from Bromley, and in London »the kids looked fabulous« (BoS 128). Both of them realised very quickly that they will not be able to go far in London with their current South London selves; they »have understood that to make it to the centre, they must develop marginal and oppositional identities. To be at the centre one must be radically marginal.«[55] At the first glance it seems paradox, but

---

49 Nahem Yousaf, *Hanif Kureishi's* The Buddha of Suburbia: *A Reader's Guide* (New York: Continuum, 2002), 40.
50 Felski, »Nothing to Declare«, 37.
51 Yousaf, *Buddha*, 32.
52 Ilona, »Buddha«, 101.
53 Ball, »The Semi-Detached Metropolis«, 15; and Procter, *Dwelling Places*, 135.
54 Ilona, »Buddha«, 101.
55 Waddick Doyle, »The Space between Identity and Otherness in Hanif Kureishi's *The Buddha of Suburbia.*« *Commonwealth Essays and Studies* 4 (1997), 113.

even the highly celebrated, ›radical‹ director Pyke is not nearly as radical as he pretends to be (cf. BoS 197). Nevertheless, his plays and the attitude he sells are extremely successful. This implies that the only chance »to get away from the drabness of the suburbs to the glittering centre of London« is to »become marginal and exotic, not suburban and peripheral but *eccentric*.«[56]

In mingling with actors, artists and upper middle class intellectuals, Karim finds his way to fulfil his personal dream of a successful London life. It is his pursuit of pleasure[57] that drives him into acting, the bohemian touch there is to it because this is what had been missing in suburbia. On the other hand, through Eva, he has ever since experienced everything bohemian as worth striving for. Frederick Holmes claims that it is »Eva and Haroon who take him [Karim] physically out of the suburbs«,[58] but in my eyes this does not go far enough. In the way Haroon and Eva enjoy their sexuality, which Karim notices more than once, they move away from the typical suburban morality and its values. Besides, it is Eva who recommends books to Karim all the time by which – together with her ›want-to-be-artsyness‹ – she fosters the bohemian attitude in him. She is the reason why Karim perceives himself as upwardly mobile and enables him to head for fame and success in England's capital although he needs to masquerade himself in order to achieve his aims.[59]

4.2 London: A Masquerade Ball?

Karim's masquerading had already started in Bromley when father and son became »faux-Indians, successfully marketing back to the English warmed-over versions of their own popular appropriations of Indian culture.«[60] Haroon uses Indian clichés for his own benefit; he does not sell Buddhism or knowledge, he only uses his Indian looks to create an identity which is not his, but merely the product of stereotypes created by his British audience. Karim, too, takes advantage of his ethnic identity: He was given the role of Mowgli in Shadwells play of *The Jungle Book*, and, as the director explicitly mentions to

56 Doyle, »Identity and Otherness«, 112.
57 Also cf.   Brian Finney, *English Fiction Since 1984: Narrating a Nation* (Basingstoke: Palgrave Macmillan, 2006), 125.
58 Frederick Holmes, »Comedy, the Carnivalesque, and the Depiction of English Society in Hanif Kureishi's *The Buddha of Suburbia* and Kingsley Amis's *Lucky Jim*.« *English Studies in Canada* 28.4 (2002), 652.
59 Also cf. Doyle, »Identity and Otherness«, 110.
60 Ball, »Semi-Detached Metropolis«, 23.

him, he was »cast for authenticity and not for experience.« (BoS 147) Besides, although being half-Indian already, he was made to »wear a loin-cloth and brown make-up, so that [he] resembled a turd in a bikini-bottom.« (BoS 146) Even though Karim did not like to be exposed in this way, he did it nonetheless as it was his only chance to star in a professional play. In other words: He used his half-Indianess to get a foot in the door of acting.

Regarding masquerading, in the *Buddha of Suburbia* much attention is given to language. When playing Mowgli, Karim is forced to use an Indian accent which his father, too, uses when doing his Buddha performance: »He was hissing his s's and exaggerating his Indian accent. He'd spent years trying to be more of an Englishmen, to be less risibly conspicuous, and now he was putting it back in spadeloads.« (BoS 21) However, not only is Karim forced into a certain kind of language, he also utilises it voluntarily for his own benefits when he decides to lose his South London accent in order »to get on.« (BoS 178) These two characters already illustrate that in the novel language is used to constitute another self, to create a certain impression and to be associated with a certain group of people, either because people want to belong to a particular party themselves or others expect them to speak like that.[61] Charlie is no exception to this rule. Being a rock star in the U.S., Americans expect him to have a strong British accent which, of course, also makes him more interesting, and, thus, he sells more records. That is why he »had acquired this cockney accent when [Karim's] first memory of him at school was that he'd cried after being mocked [...] for talking so posh. [...] Now he was going for cockney rhyming slang, too. [...] He was selling Englishness, and getting a lot of money for it.« (BoS 247) Charlie, of course, went further than only changing his accent: The whole concept of him being a punk is not genuine. Regardless that Karim thought it »artificial« to »wear rubber and safety pins«, Charlie still saw his future in it, the chance to go somewhere (BoS 131 f.).

When looking closer at the characters, almost everyone uses London as »a theatrical space where value derives not from being but from seeming«,[62] mostly with the intention of making money, and those that already have enough money try to conceal it. Shadwell and Pyke, for example, pretend to be »radical outsiders at odds with the

---

61 Also cf. Jamel Oubechou, »›The Barbarians and Philistines‹ in The Buddha of Suburbia: Dis/locating Culture«, *Commonwealth Essays and Studies* 4 (1997), 108.
62 Ball, »Semi-Detached Metropolis«, 25.

Establishment«,[63] but, actually, Pyke is absolutely wealthy with his son attending West-minster School, »one of the most expensive and exclusive in England« (BoS 197 f.). Even Eleanor, to Karim's surprise, turned out to be much more affluent than expected. Although she »dressed roughly, wearing a lot of scarves, lived in Notting Hill and – sometimes – talked with a Catford accent«, her father »was American and owned a bank; her mother was a well-respected portrait painter« and Eleanor herself »had been to country houses, to public school and Italy« (BoS 173). For this matter, in London nobody is who he or she seems to be, and only occasionally the real self shines through.

4.3 Being Oneself

Living in England leaves plenty of room for personal development, and for that reason *The Buddha of Suburbia* highlights the permeability of class divisions, which is characteristic for industrialized, western countries, especially when comparing them to countries as, for example, India. The most prominent theme is leaving the suburbs as, for instance, Eva who wants »to scour that suburban stigma right off her body«, not realising that it is »in the blood and not on the skin« (BoS 134). Suburbaness is referred to as a »stigma«, something negative that people disapprove of and, therefore, something that must be discarded. For this reason Eva puts every effort in her »rise from [a] do-it-yourself enthusiast to [a] professional interior designer«.[64]

Ted, in contrast, finds his very own self by doing the opposite, namely doing nothing. He left his former working life behind and started to enjoy his modest, but blissful, condition:

> Now Ted didn't have a bath or get up until eleven o'clock, when he read the paper until the pubs were open. The afternoons he spent out on long walks or in South London attending classes on mediation. [...] He was happy, or happier, apart from the fact that nothing in life had much meaning to him. But at least he recognized this now and was looking into it.[65]

Naturally, this behaviour of Ted outraged Jean as »they now had no income« (BoS 102). That is why she »raged and argued, and even went so far as to attempt tenderness in her effort to get Ted back to ordinary but working unhappiness.« (BoS 102)

---

63 Holmes, »Comedy«, 661.
64 Procter, *Dwelling Places*, 148.
65 BoS 102.

The younger characters of the novel approach their own identity in a slightly different way. They »enthusiastically embrace seventies' culture. Charlie turns punk [...]. Jamila joins a commune and turns lesbian. Karim [...] takes up acting in London's radical fringe theatre.«[66] They all look for an identity of their own, and an unconventional one, too.[67] While almost every protagonist in *The Buddha of Suburbia* tries to gain a better social status, which is often associated with housing, Jamila, Karim's feminist cousin, starts a dropout-like hippie life in a commune.[68] She also disapproves of Karim playing Mowgli since she perceives the play as neo-fascist and believes that Karim is reinforcing clichés by playing this role (cf. BoS 157). Of all characters she seems to be most certain of herself. »But then she has undergone the most radical transformations, from rebellious to dutiful daughter (but not wife), from militant agitator to obedient Muslim and back, and from wife in a unitary family to lesbian in a commune.«[69] This indicates that also for her it has been a long way to find out what she wants, and even her momentary situation could be considered a phase.

In contrast to Jamila, Karim and Charlie enjoy quite a high standard of living although they decided to join circles of people that are not exactly well-known for having much money: punks and experimental theatre actors. Besides, acting and making music is a field with countless competitors, so success was nothing predictable. Because the novel »traces the tenacity and continuing power of class distinctions«,[70] Karim often doubts whether it was the right choice to leave Bromley for his acting career: »I wanted to run out of this room, back to South London, where I belonged, out of which I had wrongly and arrogantly stepped.« (BoS 148) All this illustrates Karim's diversity: Sometimes he is overly confident, sometimes doubting his talents, he cannot see himself as a doctor, but neither is he quite comfortable with something more artistic. All this underlines that Kureishi's novel is a classical *bildungsroman* in which the hero of the story has to find his own identity, and even at the end we still cannot pin Karim »down as homosexual or heterosexual, as English or Indian, as true or false«.[71] If we can say something with certainty, it is that seeking a fixed identity, »whether that is national,

---

66 Finney, *English Fiction*, 125.
67 Finney, *English Fiction*, 125.
68 Wilson, »Family and Change«, 116.
69 Finney, *English Fiction*, 132.
70 Felski, »Nothing to Declare«, 38.
71 Doyle, »Identity and Otherness«, 111.

ethnic, religious, or political, is self-defeating.«[72] Anwar can be regarded evidence for that: He »appeared to be returning internally to India« (BoS 64), and he also made a decision to be strictly Muslim when he forced his daughter into arranged marriage. How self-defeating his determination was to him, is symbolised by his hunger strike during which he nearly starved himself to death. Karim, in opposite to that, enjoys not having to decide, and he even mentions that »it would be heartbreaking to have to choose one or the other« (BoS 55). Of course, this quotation only refers to his sexual preferences but applies symptomatically to most of his attitudes towards life as well. And although most characters cannot decide on their identities, have several ones or mask their real one, somehow they have found their own. It is the »[p]aradox of paradoxes: to be someone else successfully you must be yourself! This I learned!« (BoS 219 f.)

5 CONCLUSION

Summarising, it can be said that the question, whether the characters found their own selves or not, cannot be answered easily; at least, it is impossible to answer it with »yes« or »no«. What is obvious, though, is that most protagonists appear more content with their lives than at the beginning of the story, their wishes for an upper middle class life have mostly fulfilled for those who wanted to be upwardly mobile. Jamila seems happy enough with her drop-out life, and even Changez is accompanied by Shinko to the dinner at the end of the story. The necessary ›education‹ for a proper *bildungsroman* has definitely taken place. In contrast to what we experience in the novel, Rob – the narrator of Nick Hornby's *High Fidelity* – claims:

> [N]obody ever writes about how it is possible to escape and rot – how escapes can go off at half-cock, how you can leave the suburbs for the city but end up living a limp suburban life anyway. That's what happened to me; that's what happens to most people.[73]

To a certain degree, Rob proves right here: Hanif Kureishi, too, does not write about »rotting« in London. On the other hand, he is wrong because what, according to him, happens to most people, does not happen to the protagonists of *The Buddha of Suburbia* – they, indeed, find a fulfilling life in England's metropolis.

---

72 Finney, *English Fiction*, 126.
73 Nick Hornby, High Fidelity (London: Indigo, 1996), 114.

Having read the *Buddha*, the impression lingers that suburbia will never be a place to grow happy in, except for those who prefer safety and dullness. It appears a place for those that have given up to make it in the city, to make it to something grander or to prove class boundaries to be what they are: boundaries, but passable ones. London, in contrast, seems the place to be. Here it is possible to become someone else: whether fake or real does not matter since nobody is interested in that. One is who he appears to be, and at the same time will never be able to be someone else. Thus, everything seems right as long as satisfaction, pleasure and happiness is gained from it.

6 WORKS CITED

Ball, John Clement. »The Semi-Detached Metropolis: Hanif Kureishi's London.« *ARIEL*
      (A Review of International English Literature) 27.4 (1996). 7–27.

Brook, Susan. »Hedgemony?: Suburban Space in *The Buddha of Suburbia*.«. *British*
      fiction of the 1990s. Ed. Nick Bentley. London: Routledge, 2005. 209–225.

Doyle, Waddick. »The Space between Identity and Otherness in Hanif Kureishi's *The*
      Buddha of Suburbia.« *Commonwealth Essays and Studies* 4 (1997). 110–118.

Felski, Rita. »Nothing to Declare: Identity, Shame, and the Lower Middle Class.«
      Publications of the Modern Language Association of America 115.1 (2000). 33–45.

Finney, Brian. *English Fiction Since 1984: Narrating a Nation*. Basingstoke: Palgrave
      Macmillan, 2006.

Hartley, John. *Popular Reality: Journalism, Modernity, Popular Culture*. London: Arnold,
      1996.

Holmes, Frederick. »Comedy, the Carnivalesque, and the Depiction of English Society in
      Hanif Kureishi's *The Buddha of Suburbia* and Kingsley Amis's *Lucky Jim*.« *English*
      Studies in Canada 28.4 (2002). 645–666.

Hornby, Nick: *High Fidelity*. London: Indigo, 1996.

Ilona, Anthony. »Hanif Kureishi's *Buddha of Suburbia*: ›A New Way of Being British‹.«
      Contemporary British fiction. Ed. Richard Lane et al. Cambridge: Polity Press,
      2003. 87–105.

Kureishi, Hanif. The Buddha of Suburbia. London: Faber and Faber, 1990.

Oubechou, Jamel. »›The Barbarians and Philistines‹ in *The Buddha of Suburbia*:
      Dis/locating Culture.« *Commonwealth Essays and Studies* 4 (1997). 101–109.

Procter, James. *Dwelling Places: Postwar Black British Writing*. Manchester:
      Manchester Univ. Press, 2003.

Reid, Ivan. *Class in Britain*. Malden, Mass.: Polity Press, 1998.

Roberts, Kenneth. *Class in Modern Britain*. Basingstoke: Palgrave, 2001.

Wilson, Janet. »The Family and Change: Contemporary Second-Generation British-Asian
      Fiction.« *CDS Research Report* 23 (2005). 109–120.

Yousaf, Nahem. *Hanif Kureishi's The Buddha of Suburbia: A Reader's Guide*. New York:
      Continuum, 2002.